NATIONAL GEOGRAPHIC

D0503605

What Shapes Do You See?

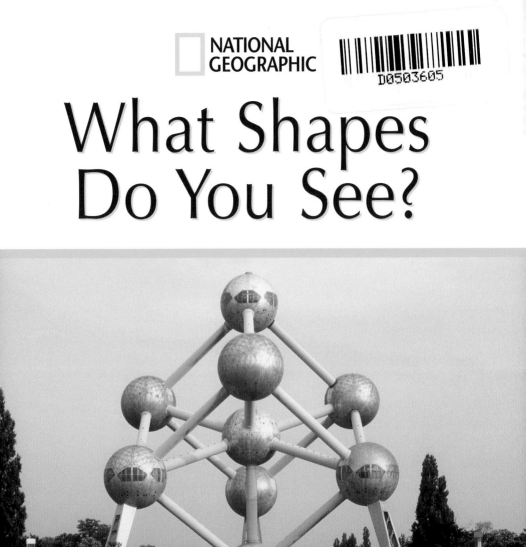

Matthew Taylor

Look at the shapes.

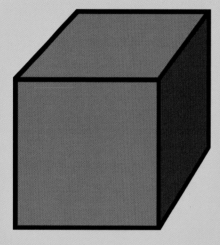

cube

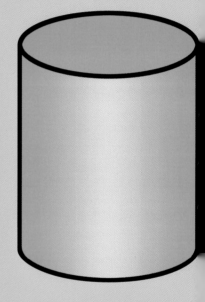

cylinder

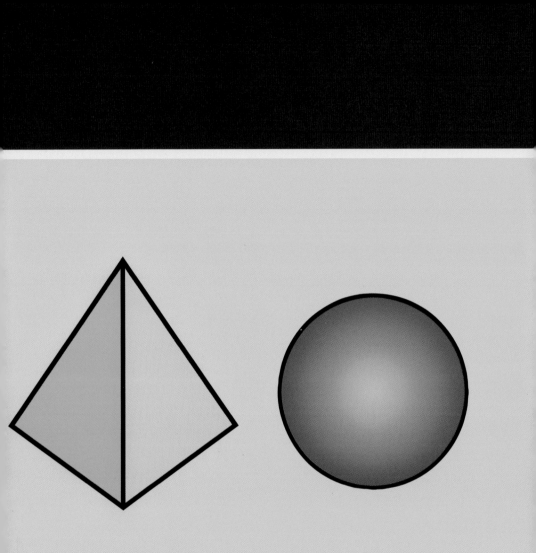

pyramid   sphere

3

What shape do you see?

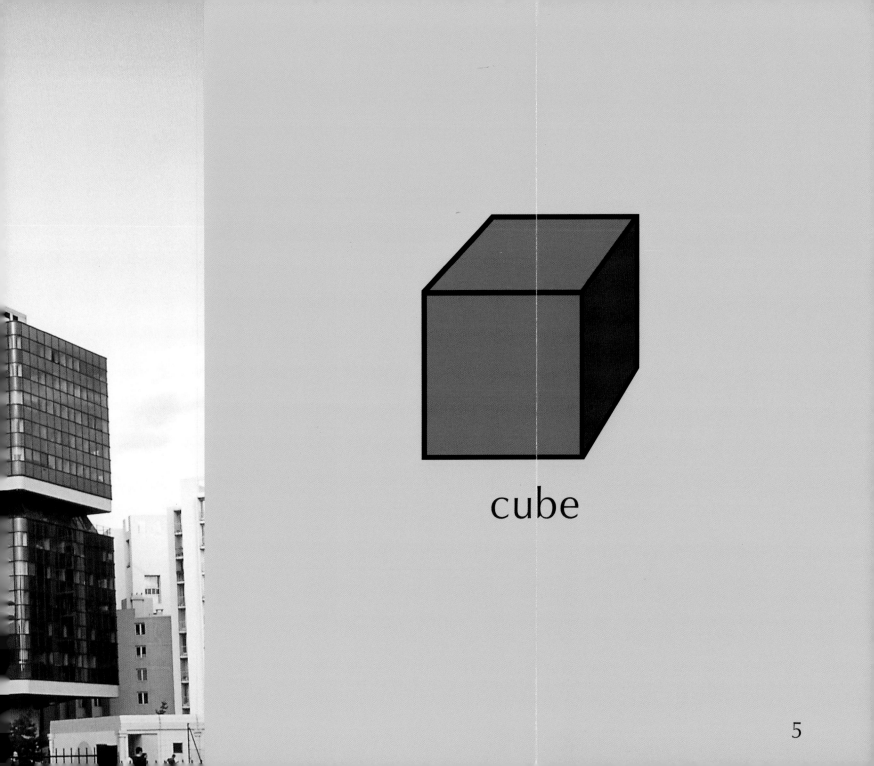

cube

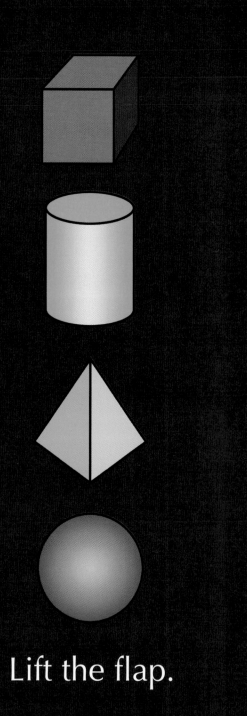

Lift the flap.

What shape do you see?

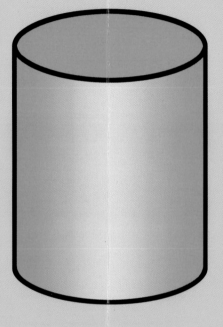

cylinder

What shape do you see?

Lift the flap.

8

pyramid

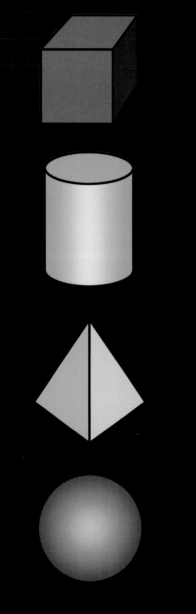

Lift the flap.

What shape do you see?

sphere

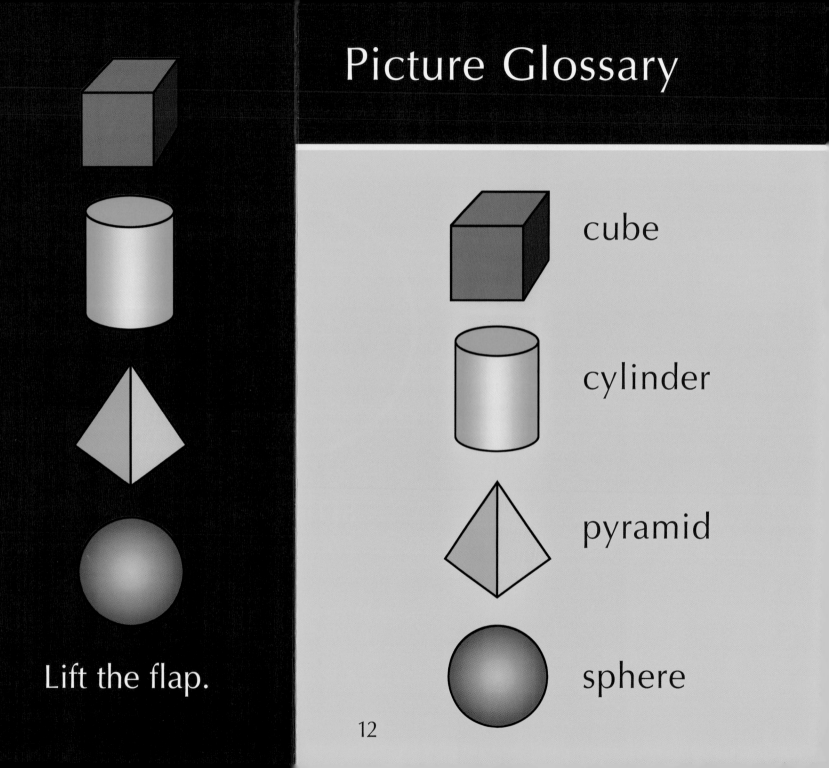

Picture Glossary

Lift the flap.

cube

cylinder

pyramid

sphere